How to Draw Airplanes Step-by-Step Guide

Best Airplane Drawing Book for You and Your Kids

BY

ANDY HOPPER

Copyright Notes

Table of Contents

Introduction

Kids have this intense desire to express themselves the ways they know how to. During their formative years, drawing all sorts is on top of their favorite things to do. You ought to encourage as it boosts their creativity and generally advances their cognitive development.

This book is written to give you and your kids the smoothest drawing experience with the different guides and instructions on how to draw different kinds of objects and animals. However, you should note that drawing, like everything worthwhile, requires a great deal of patience and consistency. Be patient with your kids as they wade through the tips and techniques in this book and put them into practice. Now, they will not get everything on the first try, but do not let this deter them. Be by their side at every step of the way and gently encourage them. In no time, they will be perfect little creators, and you, their trainer.

Besides, this is a rewarding activity to do as it presents you the opportunity of hanging out with your kids and connecting with them in ways you never knew was possible. The book contains all the help you need, now sit down with them and help them do this.

That is pretty much all about it - we should start this exciting journey now, shouldn't we?

How to draw Airplane1

Step 1.

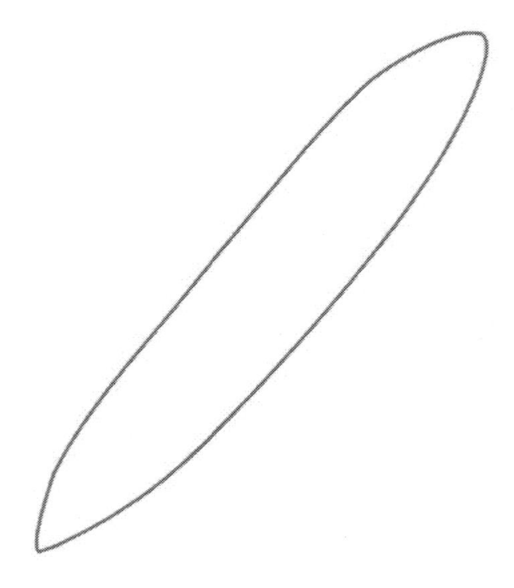

Draw an elongated oval from the top right corner of the sheet to the bottom left.

Step 2.

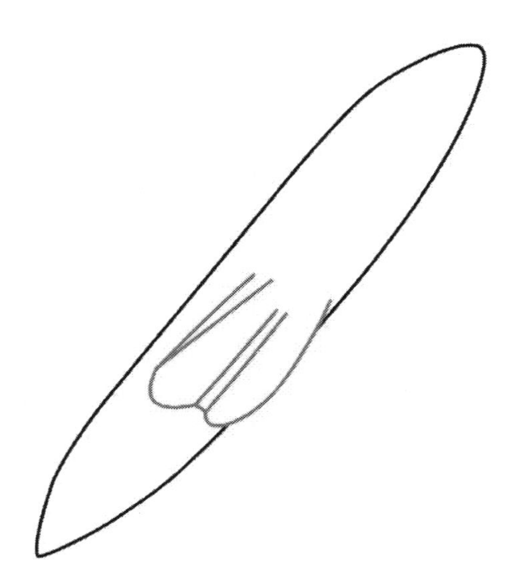

Draw the bottom of the plane, as shown in the example.

Step 3.

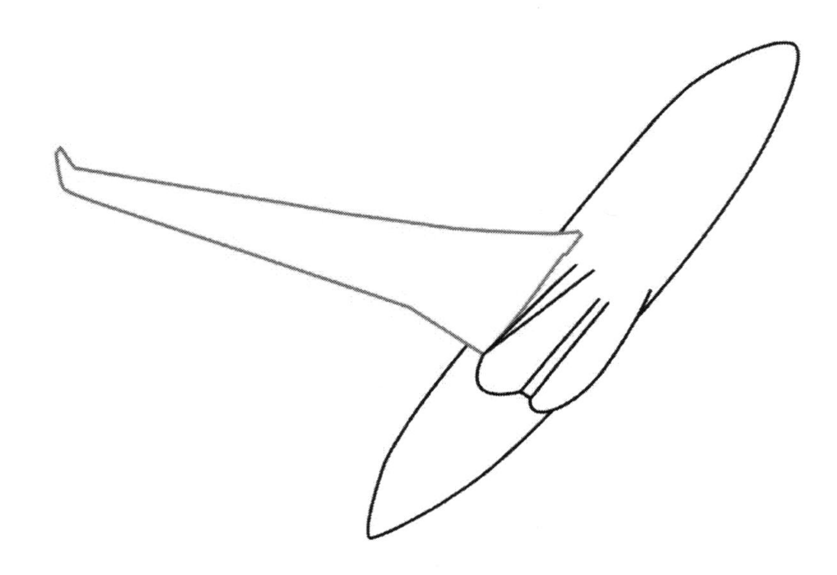

Draw on the left an extended triangular wing with an upturned end.

Step 4.

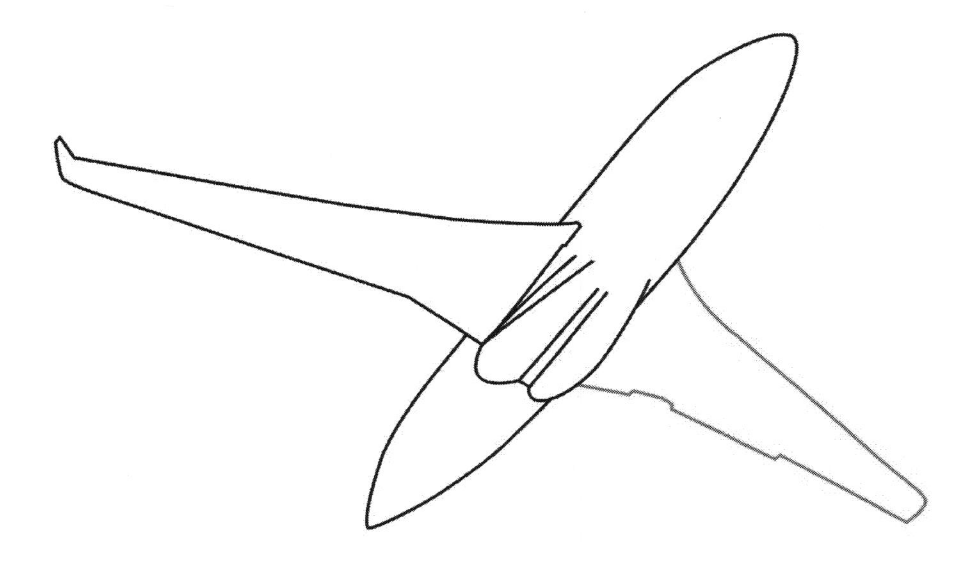

Draw on the right the same wing.

Step 5.

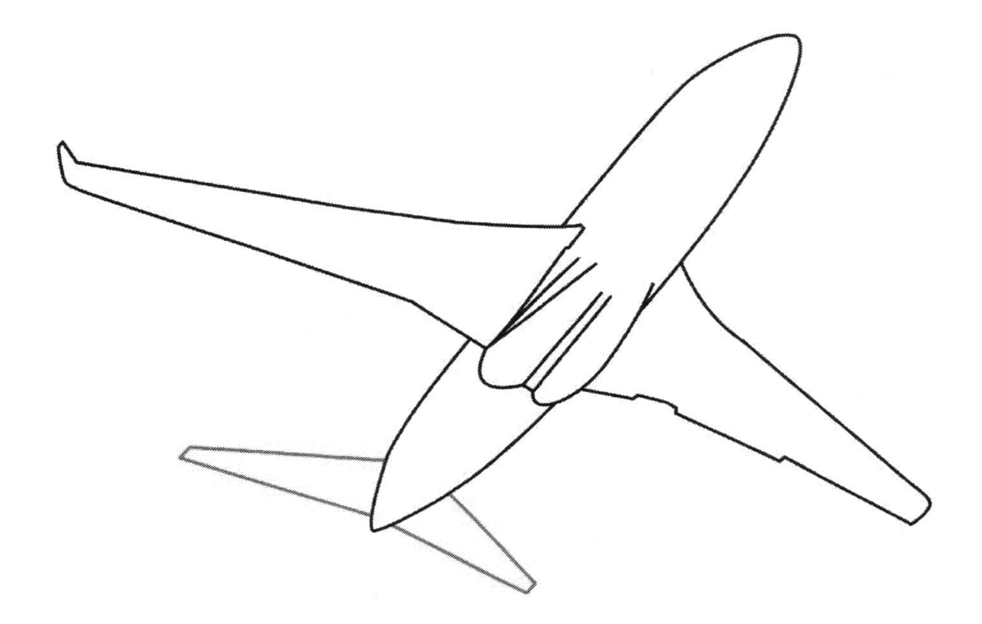

Add a tail to the plane with the help of two middle triangles.

Step 6.

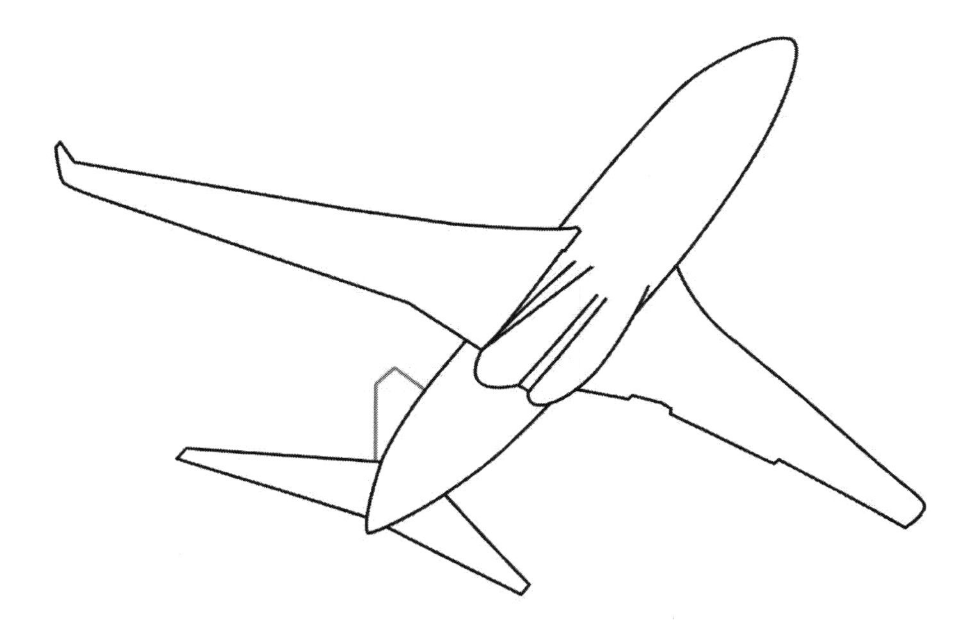

Add a keel on the back of the airplane.

Step 7.

Draw two large round engines on the wings of an airplane.

Step 8.

Add three extruded elements to the back of both wings.

Step 9.

Draw spoilers and flaps, holes for the airplane and a couple of other elements of the airplane, as shown in the example.

Step 10.

Draw a side window and a door, add a few strips to decorate the airplane.

Step 11.

Done, let's start coloring!

Step 12.

Color picture using blue for body and turbines, grey for wings and tail, red and yellow for decor.

Step 13.

Add some shadows and highlights to add volume.

Step 14.

Colored version.

How to draw Airplane2

Step 1.

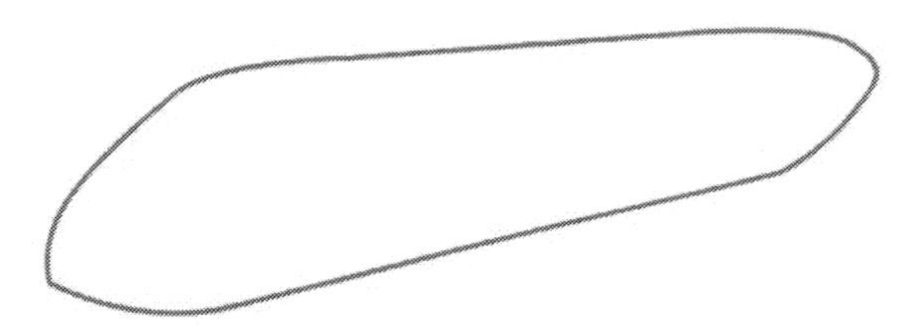

Draw an elongated oval for the body of the airplane, more voluminous on the left side.

Step 2.

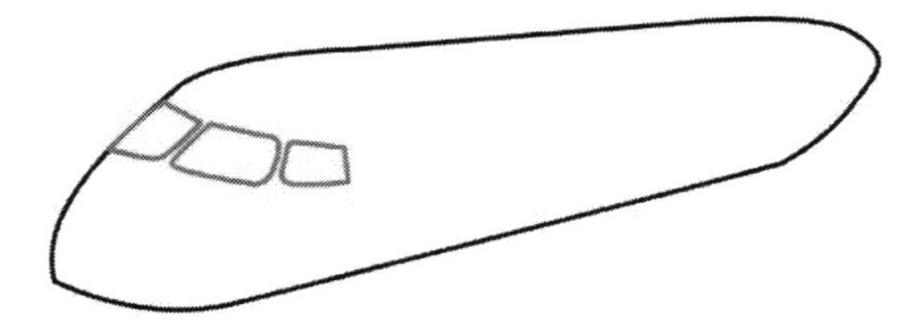

Draw the cockpit windows.

Step 3.

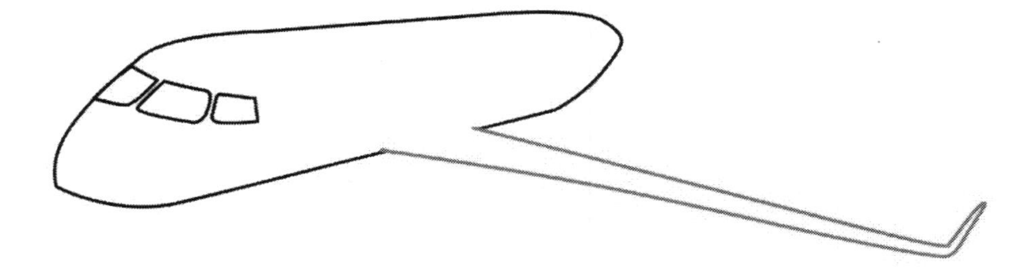

Add to the right a narrow long wing with a curved end.

Step 4.

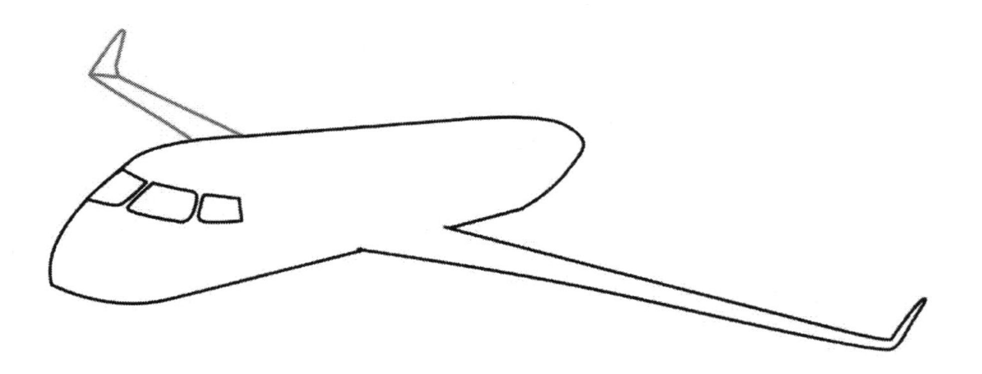

Add to the left the same wing a little shorter.

Step 5.

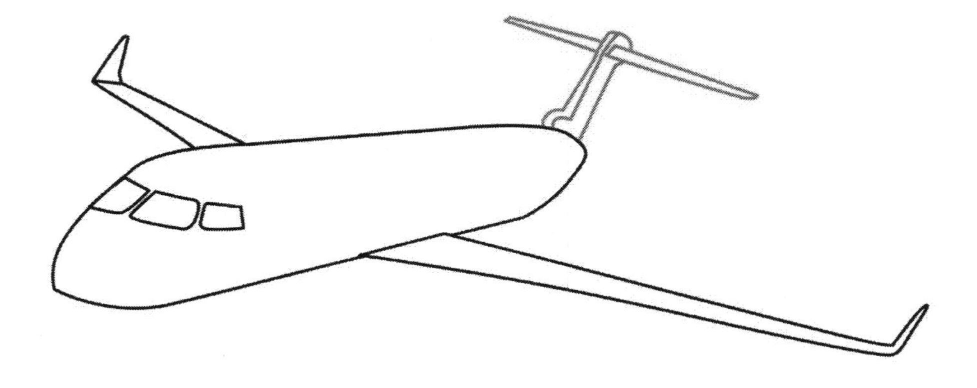

Draw the tail of the airplane, as shown in the example.

Step 6.

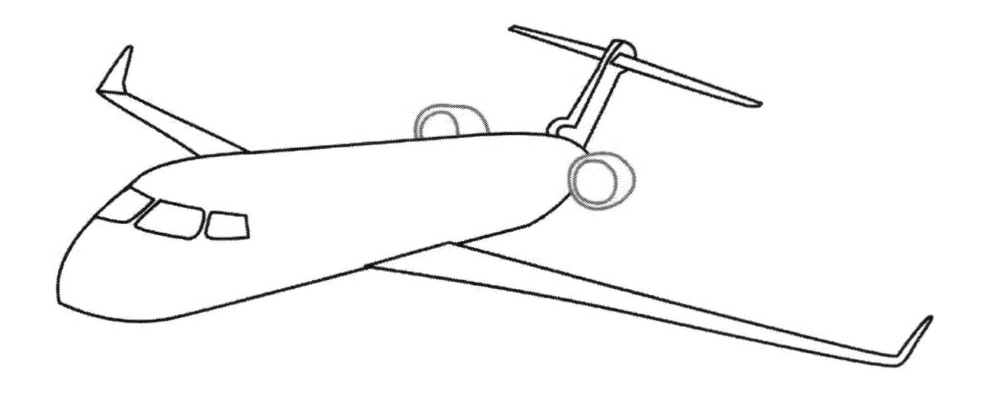

Draw two round engines on the right and left side of the tail section of the airplane.

Step 7.

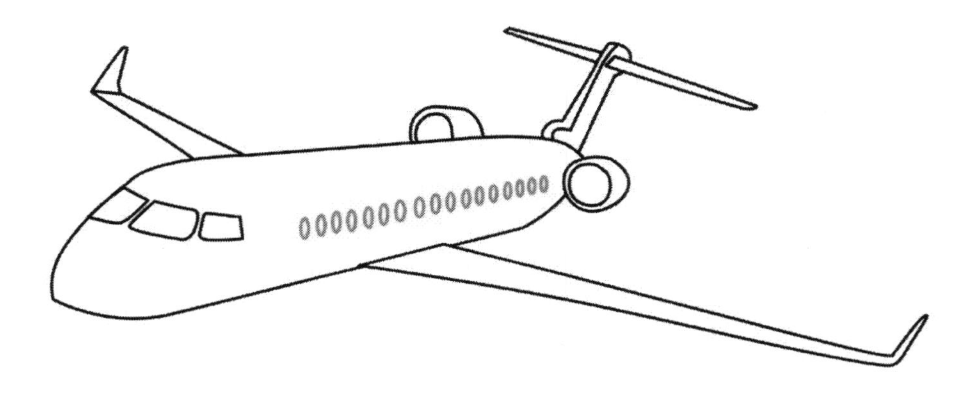

Add small round portholes along the entire airplane.

Step 8.

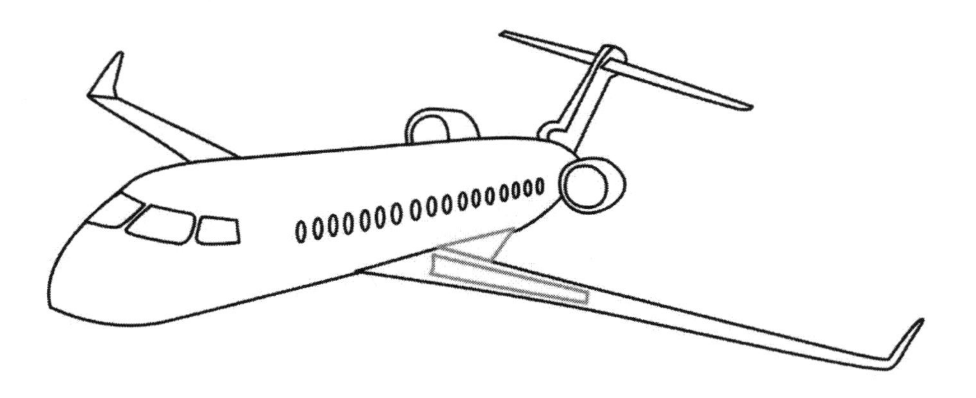

Add flap lines to the right wing.

Step 9.

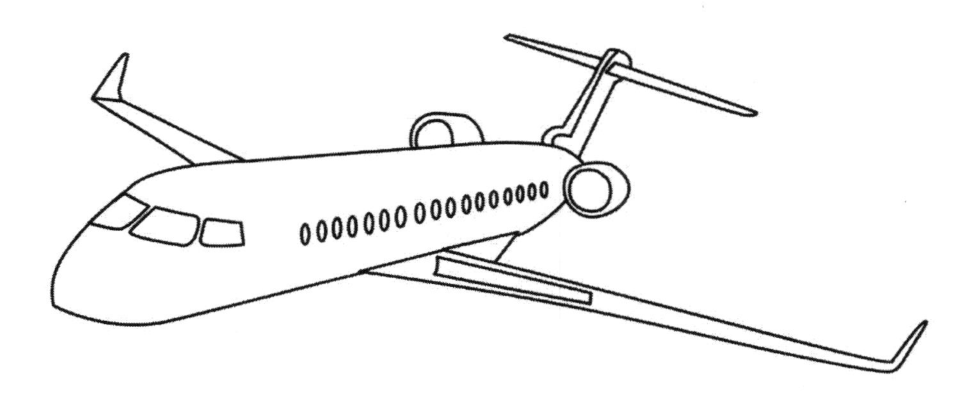

Done, let's start coloring!

Step 10.

Color picture using grey for body, black for windows and turbines interior.

Step 11.

Add some shadows and highlights to add volume.

Step 12.

Colored version.

How to draw Airplane3

Step 1.

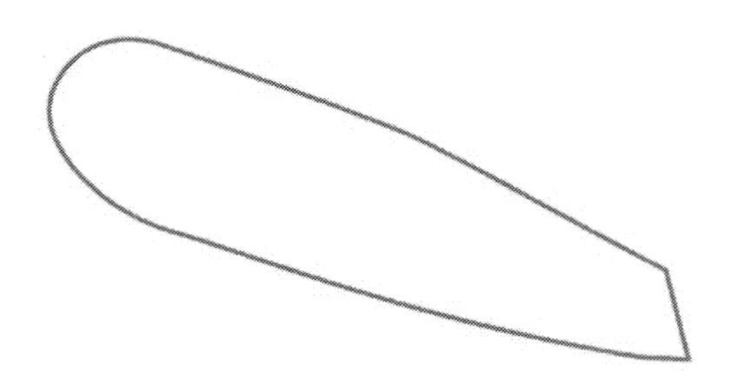

Draw a horizontal elongated oval shape in the middle of the sheet with a slight inclination to the right.

Step 2.

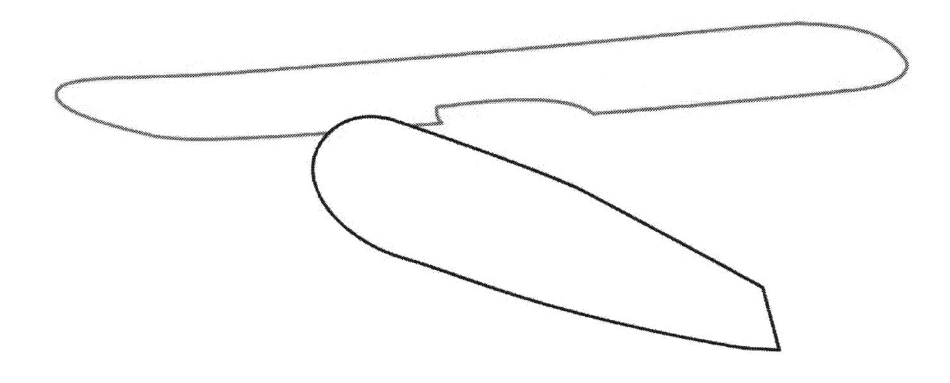

Add the upper wings above the figure, be close to the original.

Step 3.

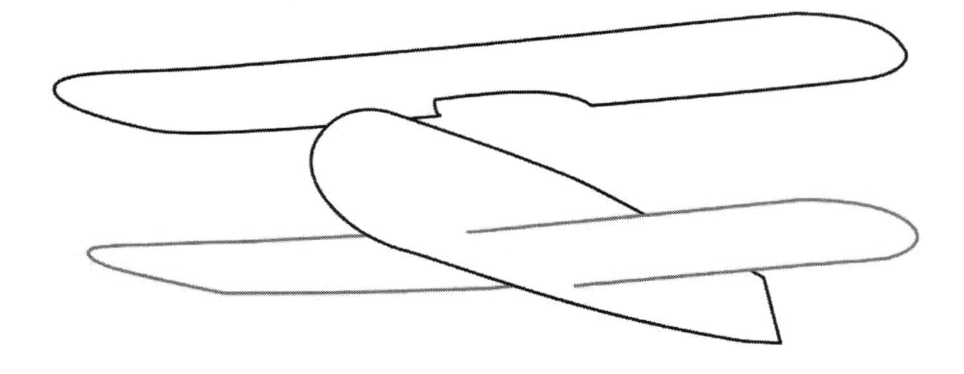

Add the lower wings under the figure.

Step 4.

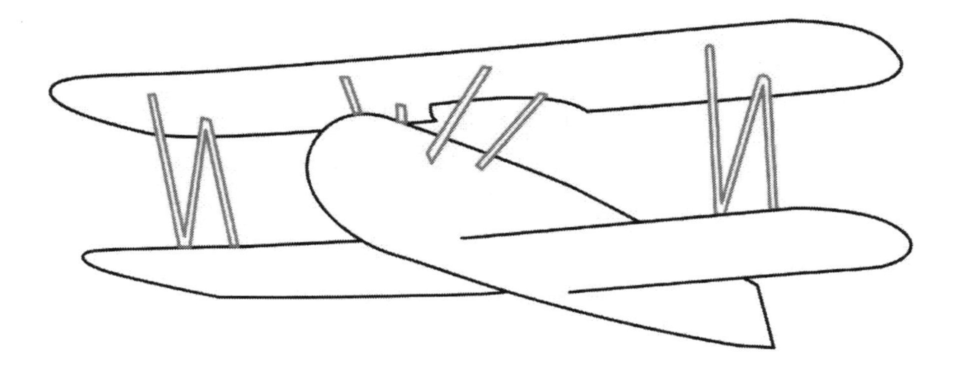

Connect the upper and lower wings with straight lines, as shown in the example.

Step 5.

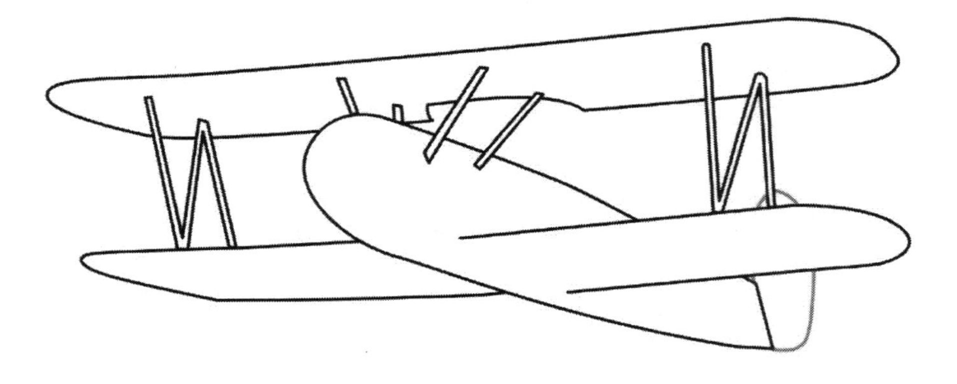

Add a vertical part of the tail to the right.

Step 6.

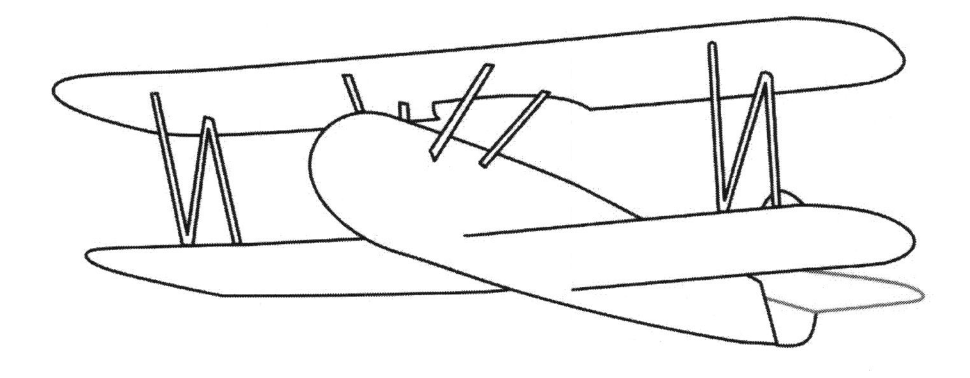

Add the horizontal part of the tail to the right.

Step 7.

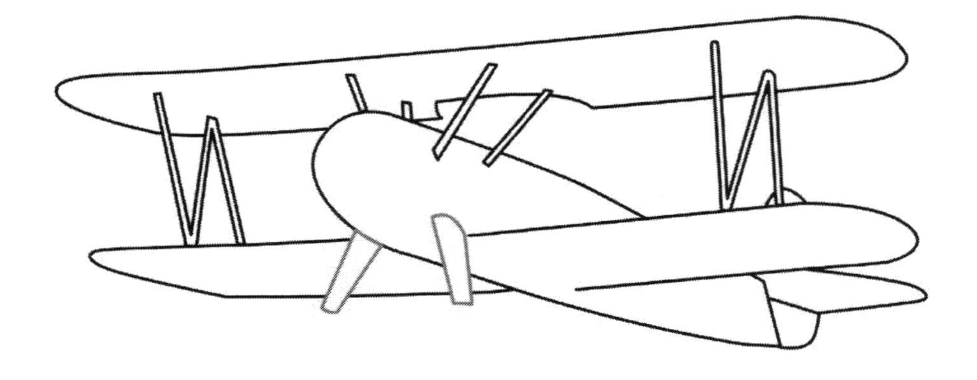

Draw two racks of the chassis.

Step 8.

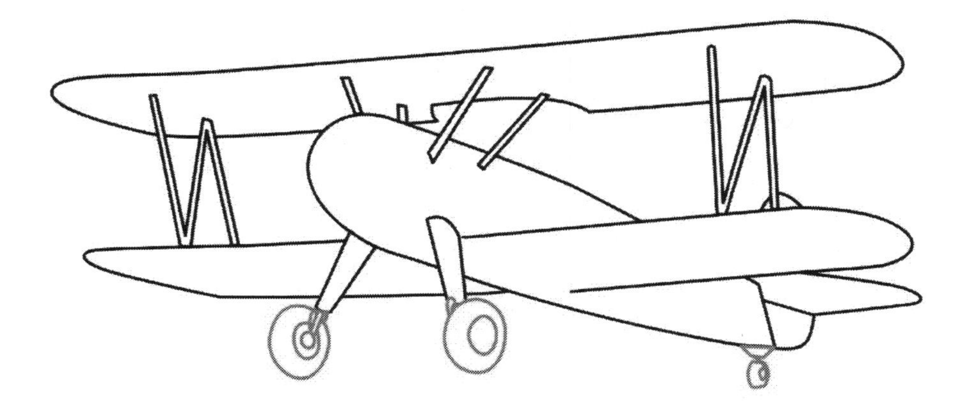

Draw three wheels - two in front and one in the tail.

Step 9.

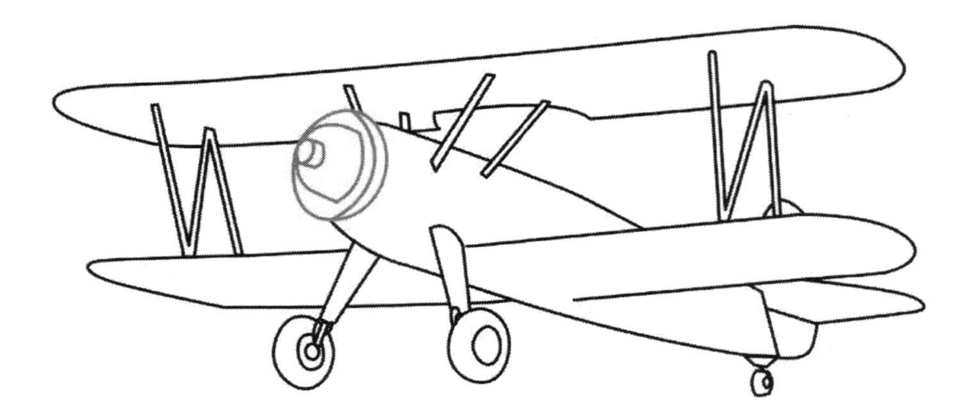

Draw a nose, as shown in the example.

Step 10.

Add a screw to the nose.

Step 11.

Done, let's start coloring!

Step 12.

Color picture using yellow for body, black for wheels and a circle around propeller, blue for tail, red for decor.

Step 13.

Add some shadows and highlights to add volume.

Step 14.

Colored version.

How to draw Airplane4

Step 1.

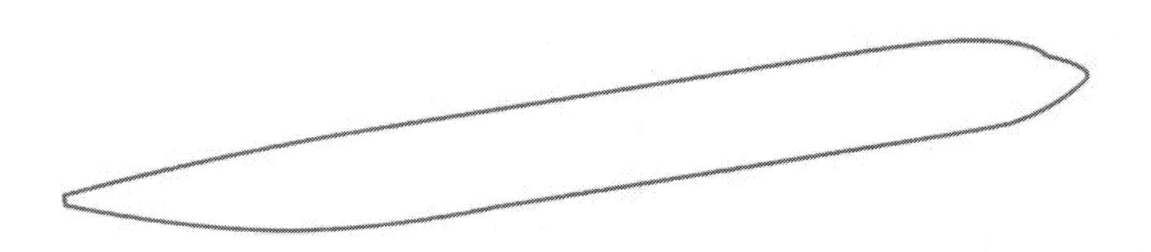

Draw an elongated horizontal oval with a slight inclination to the left.

Step 2.

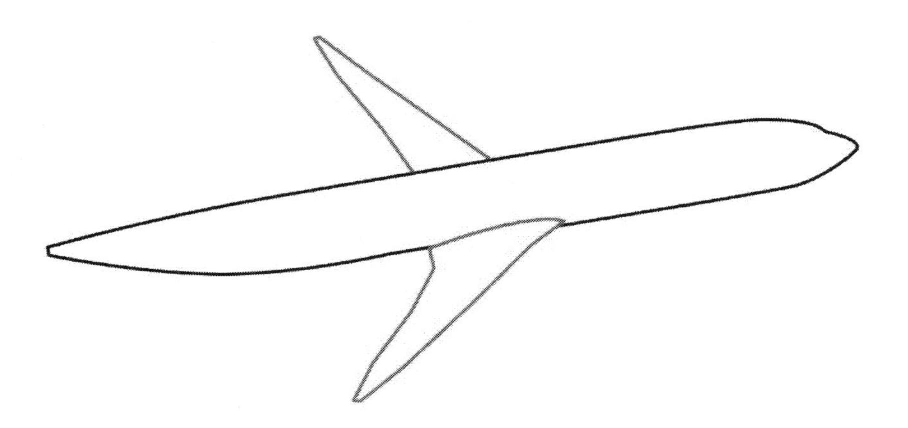

Draw two triangular wings above and below as shown in the example.

Step 3.

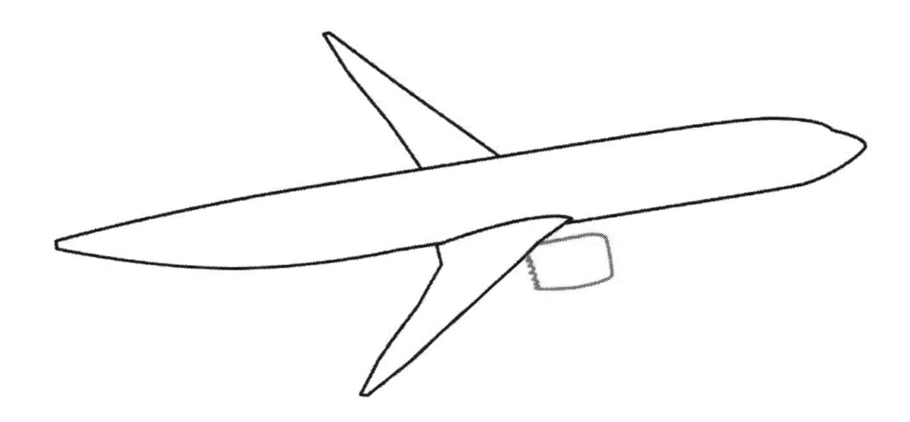

Draw a turbine between the hull and the lower wing.

Step 4.

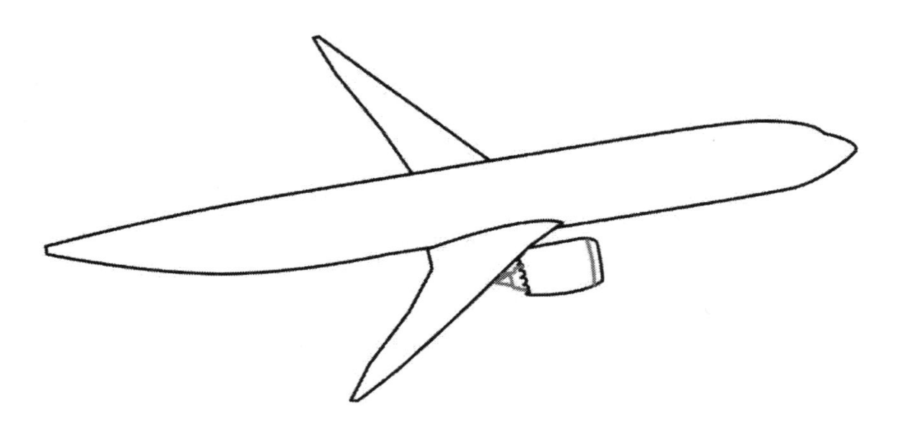

Add mounting parts and internal parts of the turbine.

Step 5.

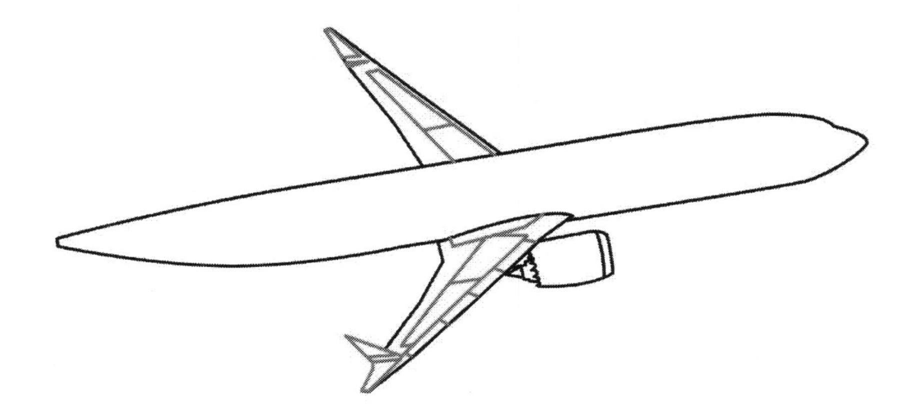

Add strips to the wings for flaps and spoilers.

Step 6.

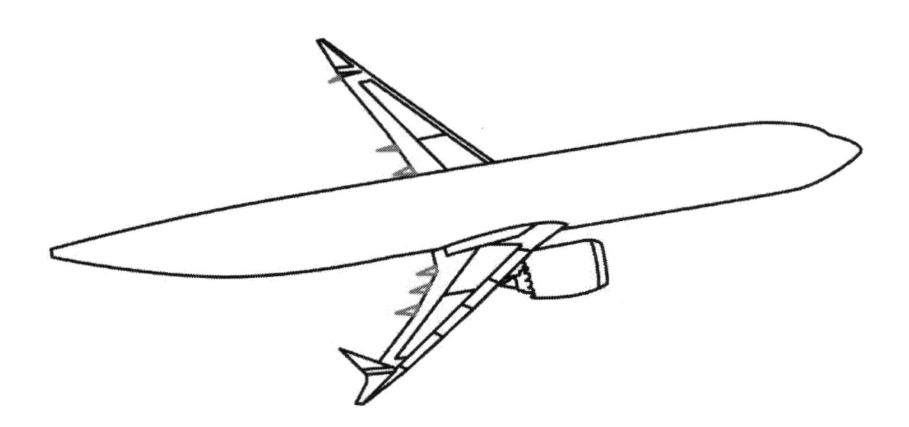

Draw small triangles on the rear edges of the wings.

Step 7.

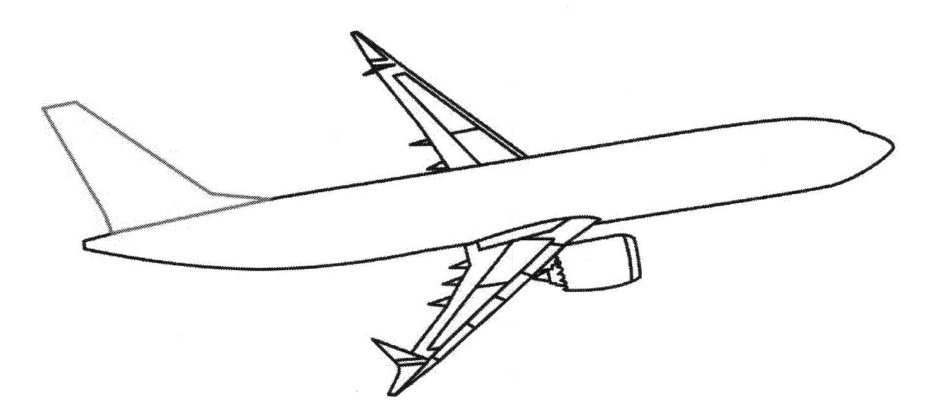

Draw the plane keel.

Step 8.

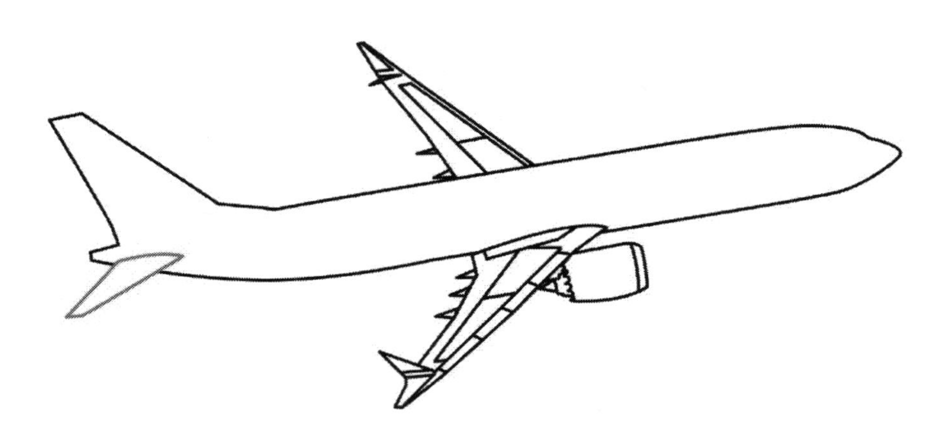

Add the tail on the left side of the airplane.

Step 9.

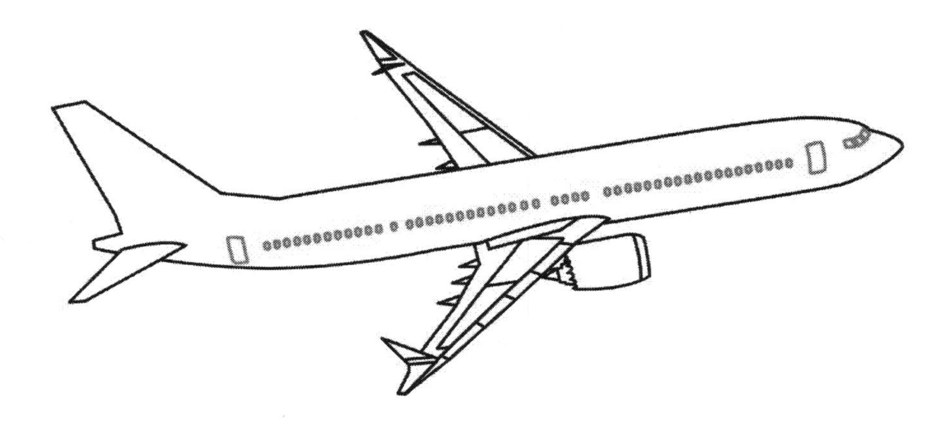

Draw portholes along the entire airplane, as well as the cockpit windows and two doors at the beginning and end of the hull.

Step 10.

Add lines to the body and tail of the airplane for decoration.

Step 11.

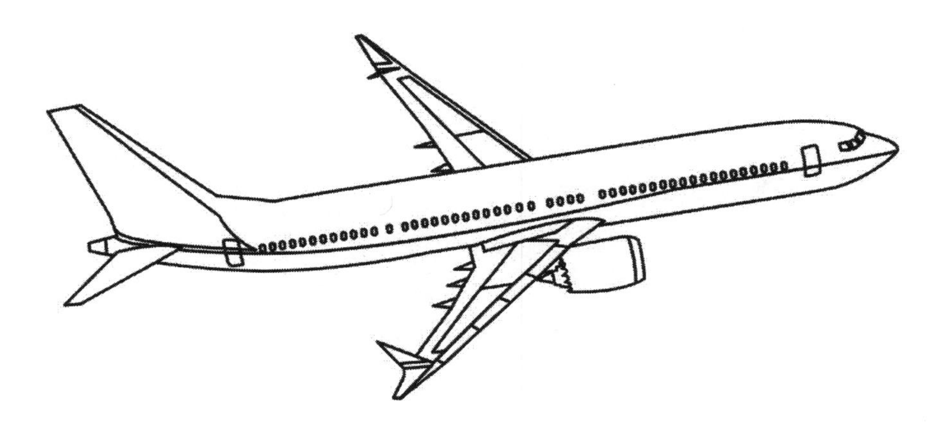

Done, let's start coloring!

Step 12.

Color picture using white for body and turbine, blue for tail and grey for belly and wings.

Step 13.

Add some shadows and highlights to add volume.

Step 14.

Colored version.

How to draw Airplane5

Step 1.

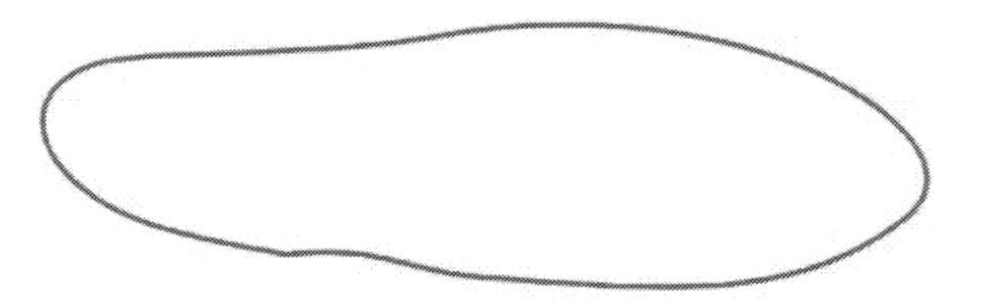

Draw a horizontal oval shape in the center of the sheet.

Step 2.

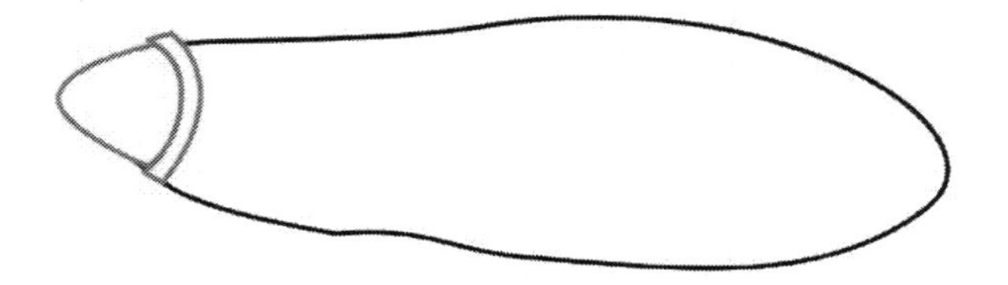

Draw a nose on the left side.

Step 3.

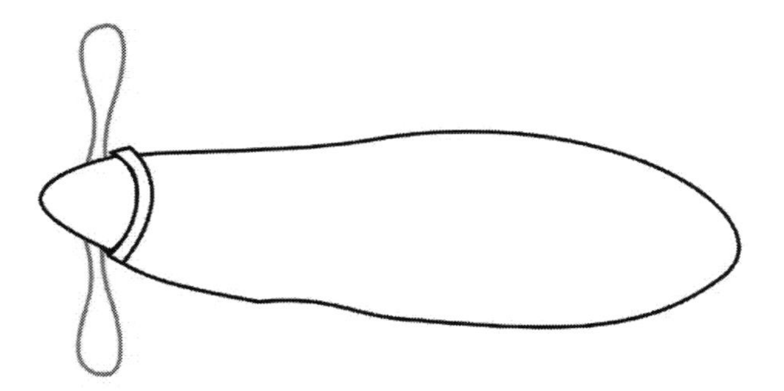

Add a screw to the nose of the airplane.

Step 4.

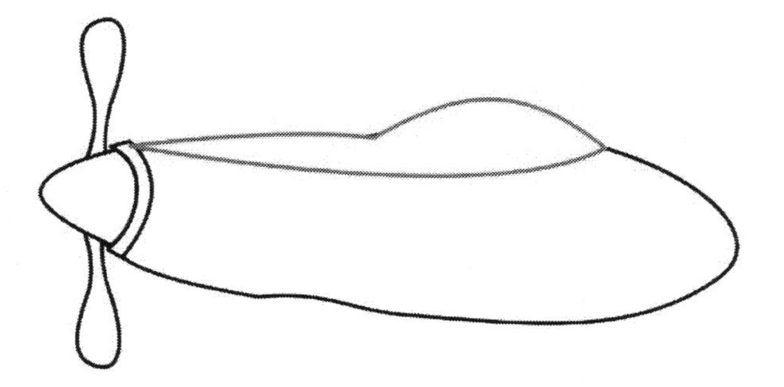

Draw a pylon cabin at the top of the hull.

Step 5.

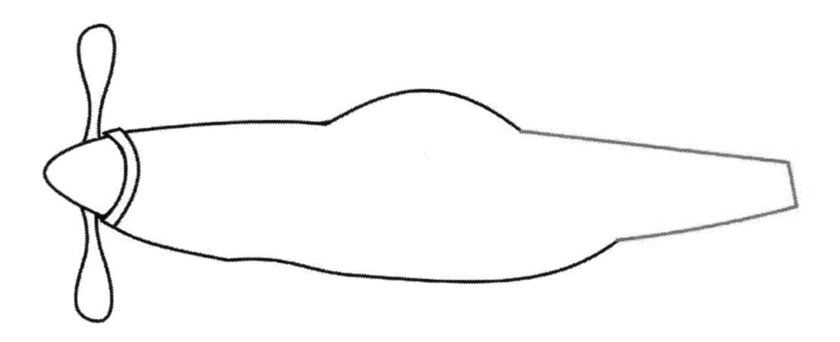

Remove the extra lines and add the back of the airplane.

Step 6.

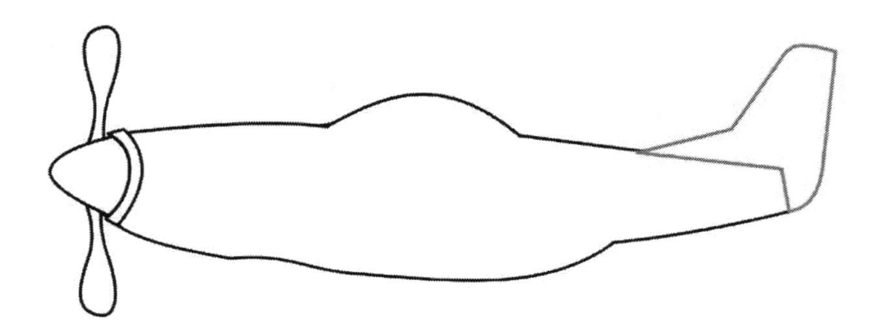

Draw the keel on the right side of the figure.

Step 7.

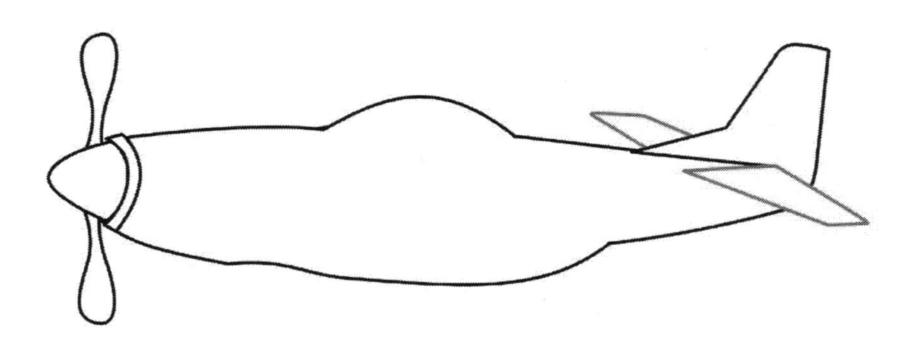

Add tails on both sides of the keel.

Step 8.

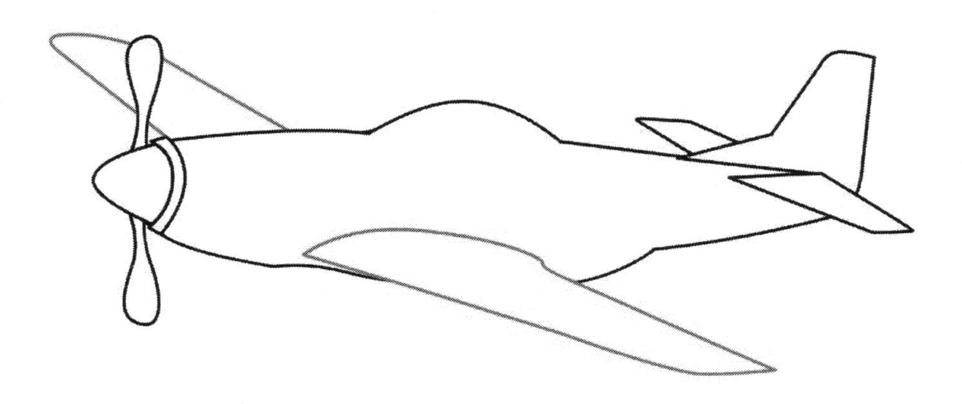

Draw the elongated wings of the airplane.

Step 9.

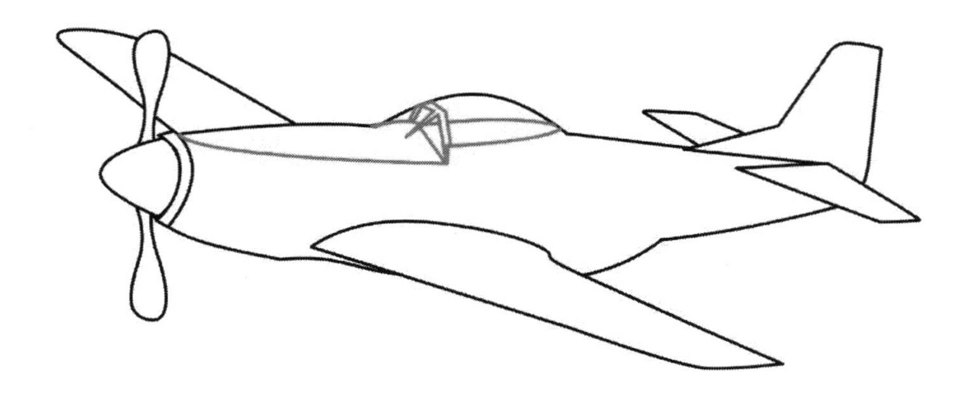

Add to the cockpit depth and volume using several lines, as shown in the example.

Step 10.

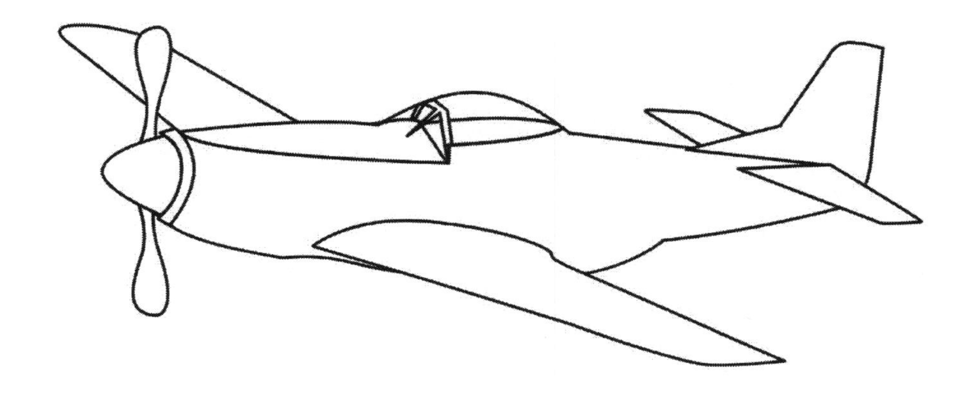

Done, let's start coloring!

Step 11.

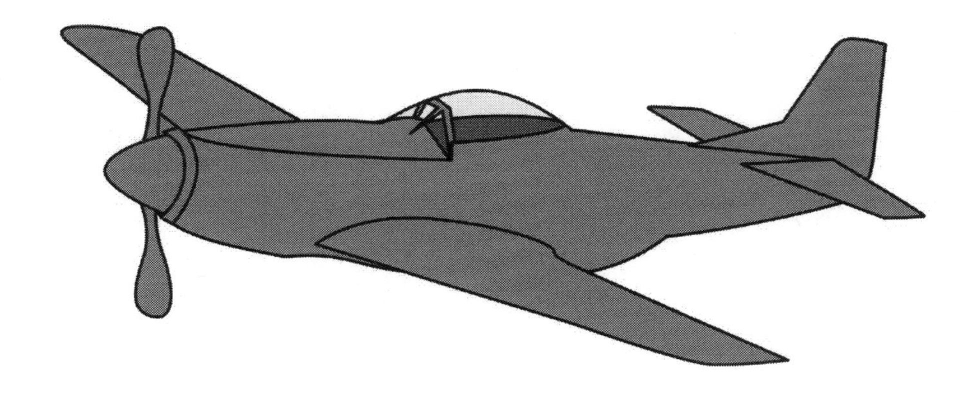

Color picture using grey for body and red for decor.

Step 12.

Add some shadows and highlights to add volume.

Step 13.

Colored version.

How to draw Airplane6

Step 1.

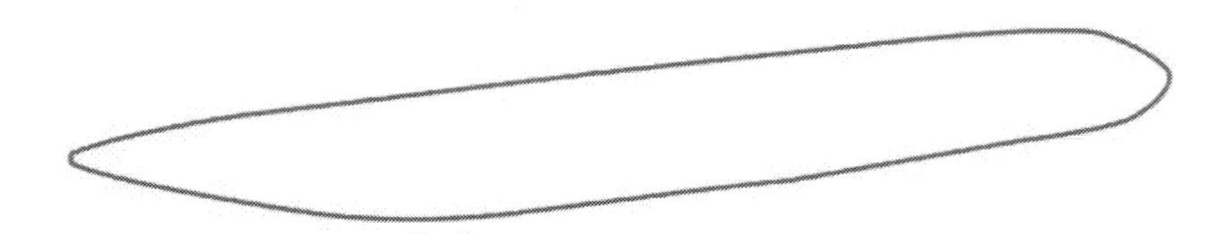

Draw an elongated horizontal oval with a slight inclination to the left.

Step 2.

Add a triangular keel on the left side.

Step 3.

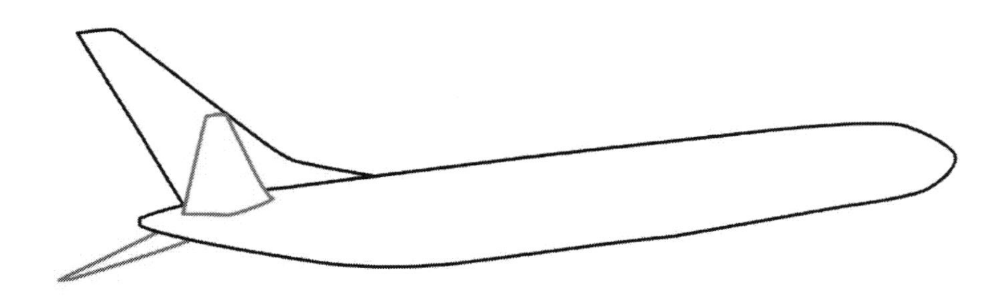

Draw the tail with two triangles on either side of the keel.

Step 4.

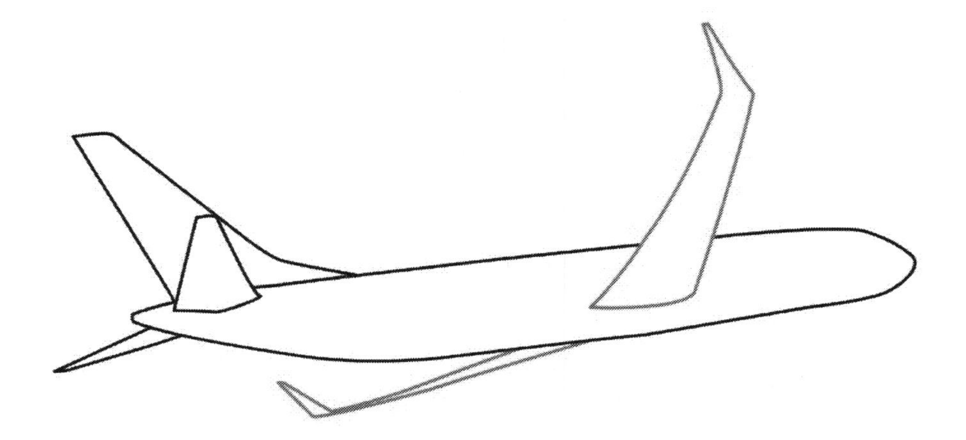

Draw elongated narrow wings with ends curled up.

Step 5.

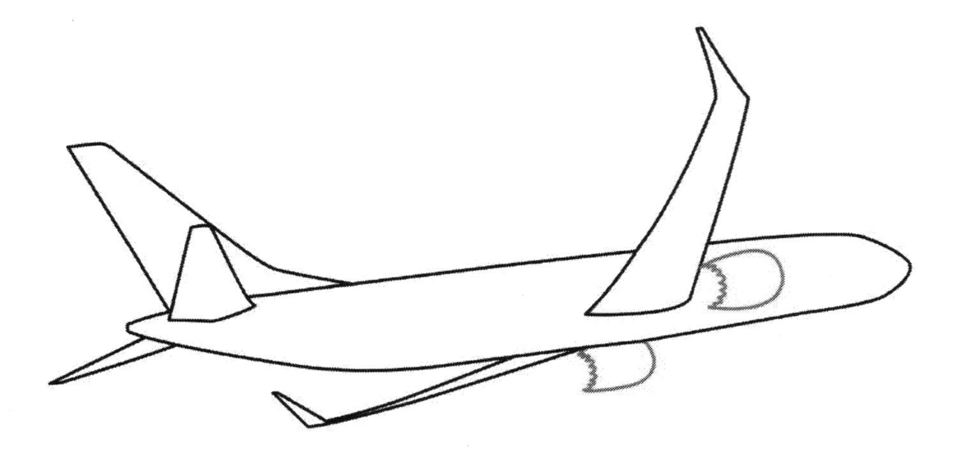

Add two turbines in front of the wings.

Step 6.

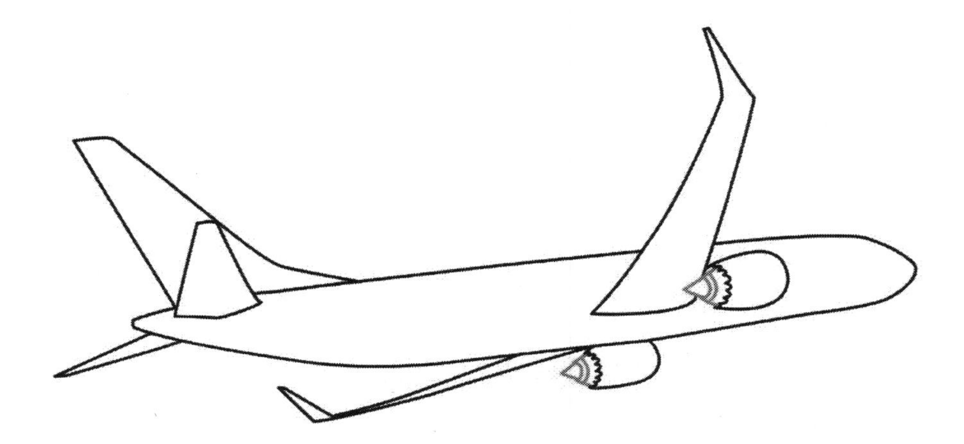

Draw the internal parts of the turbines.

Step 7.

Add oval parts on the wings.

Step 8.

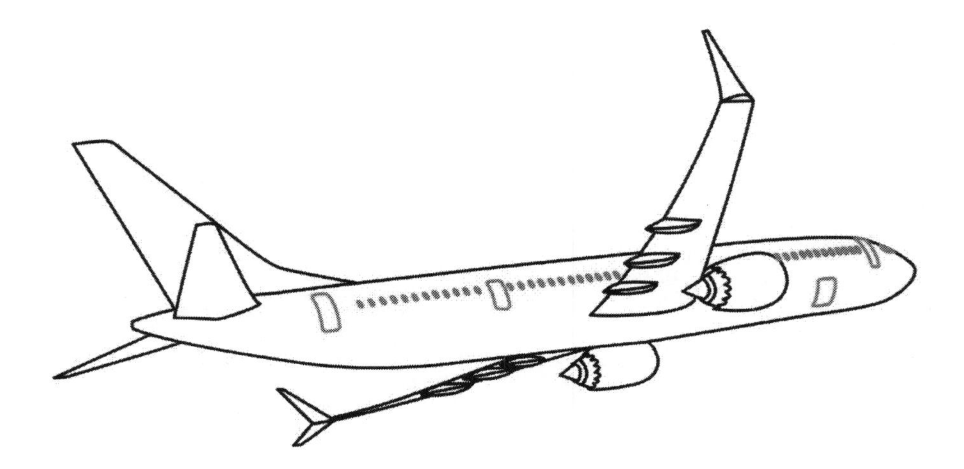

Draw portholes and doors along the entire body.

Step 9.

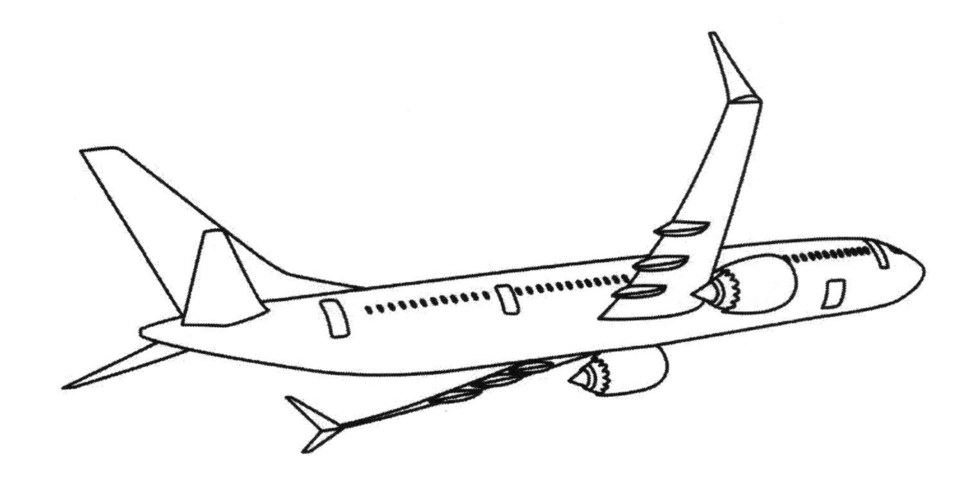

Done, let's start coloring!

Step 10.

Color picture using red and white for body and grey for tail and wings.

Step 11.

Add some shadows and highlights to add volume.

Step 12.

Colored version.

How to draw Airplane7

Step 1.

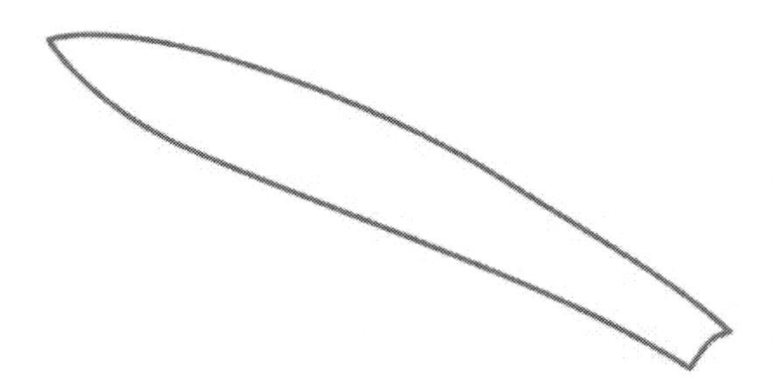

Draw an elongated shape with a slope to the right, as shown in the example.

Step 2.

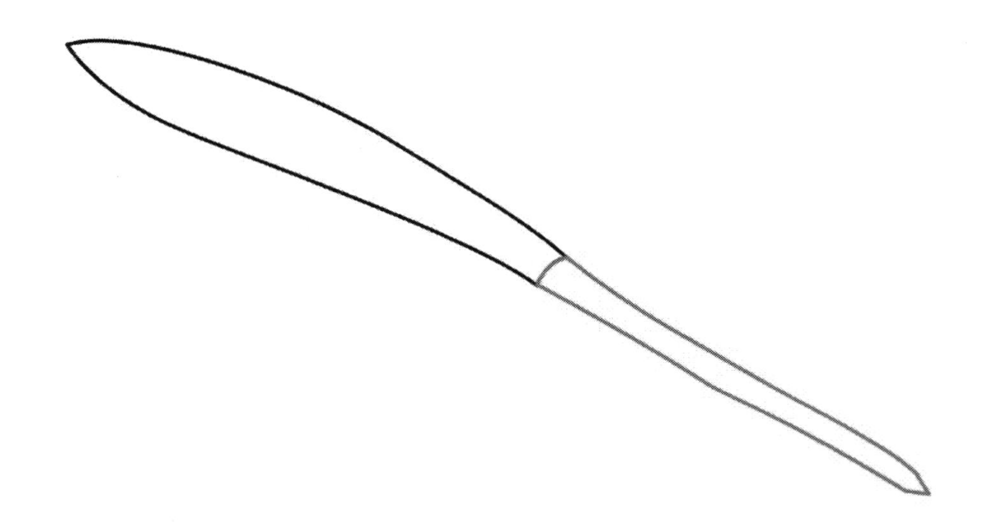

Add to the figure a thin elongated part on the right side.

Step 3.

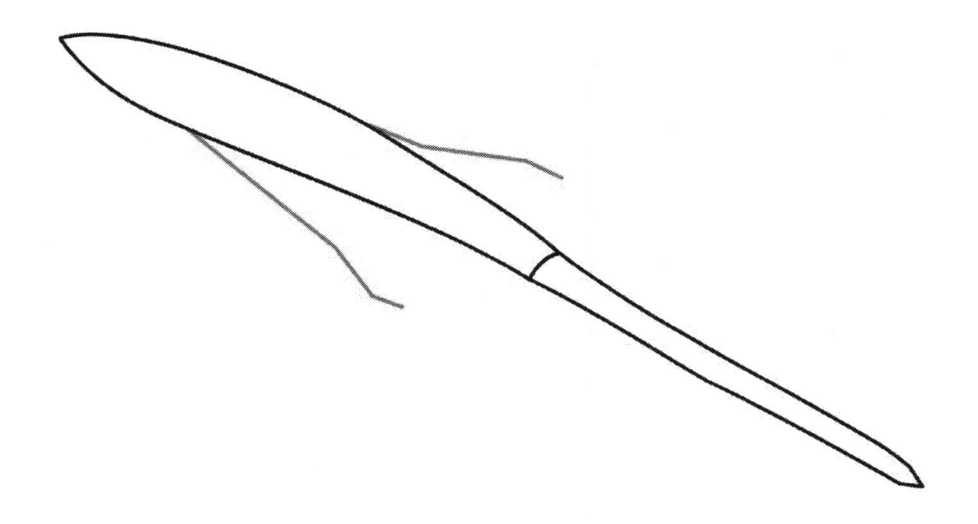

Draw two lines running from the center of the first figure at a slight angle from the body to the side.

Step 4.

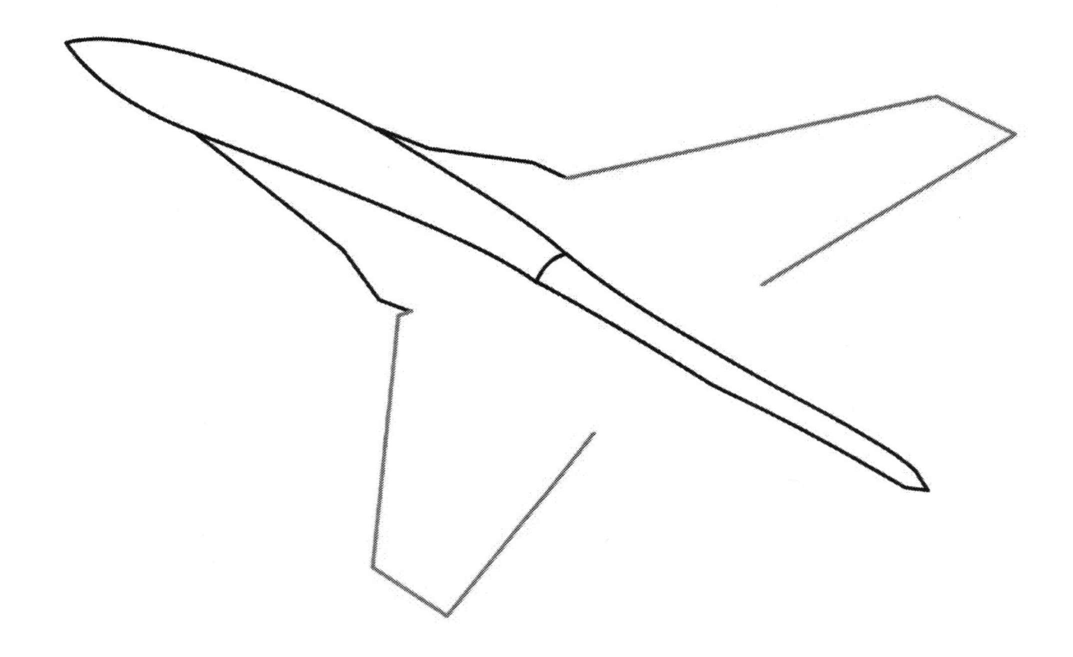

Draw wide wings on both sides of the body, be close to the original.

Step 5.

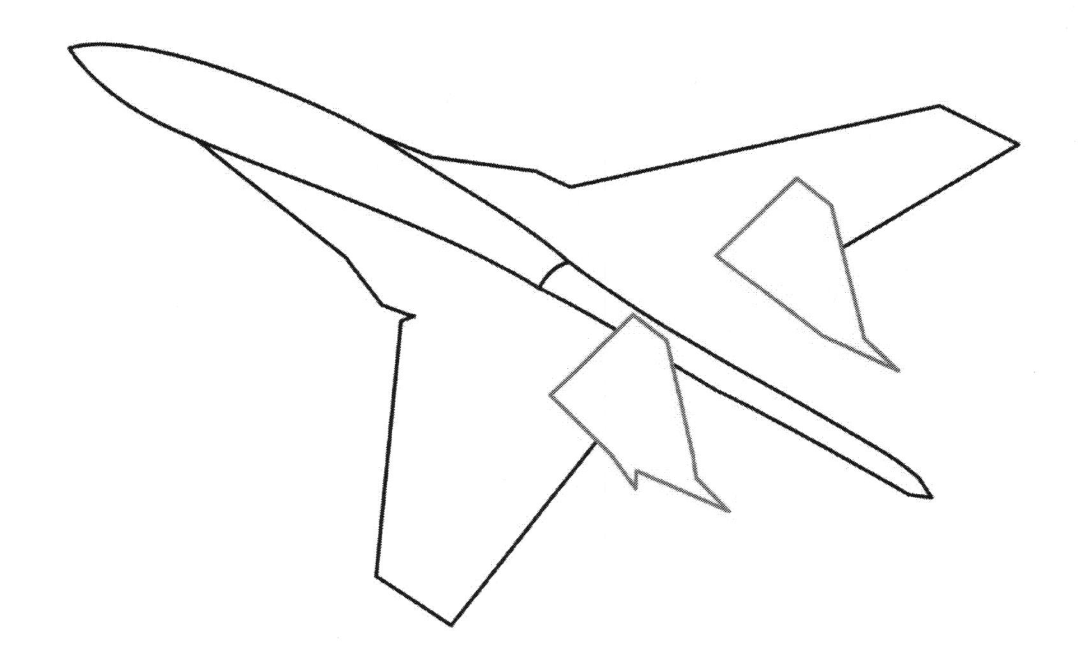

Draw tail vertical triangular pieces, as shown in the example.

Step 6.

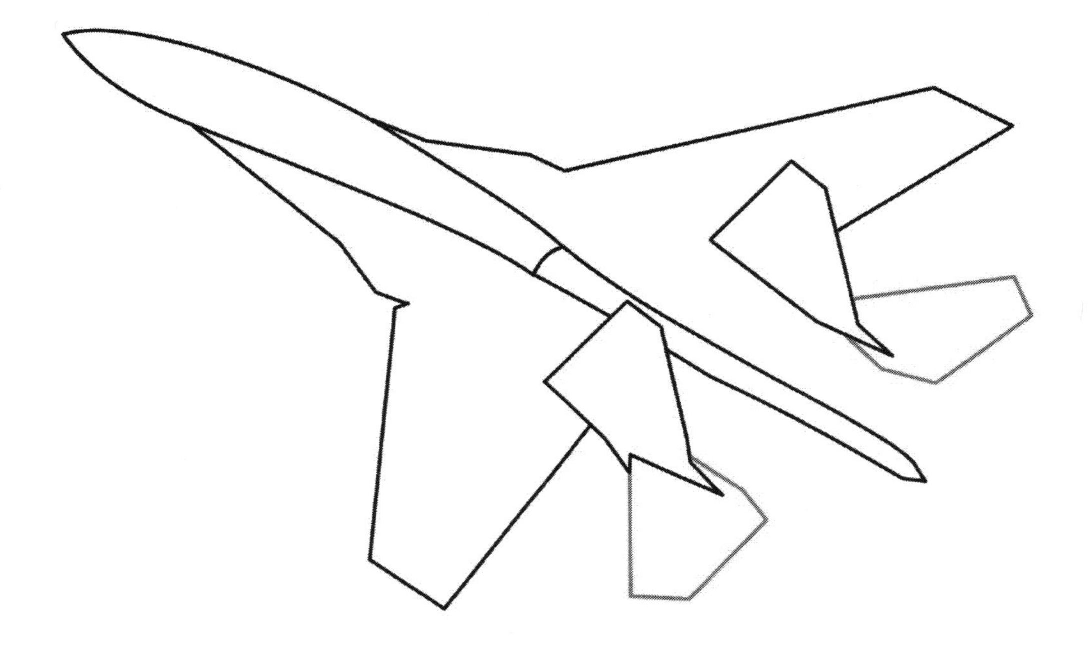

Add horizontal tails.

Step 7.

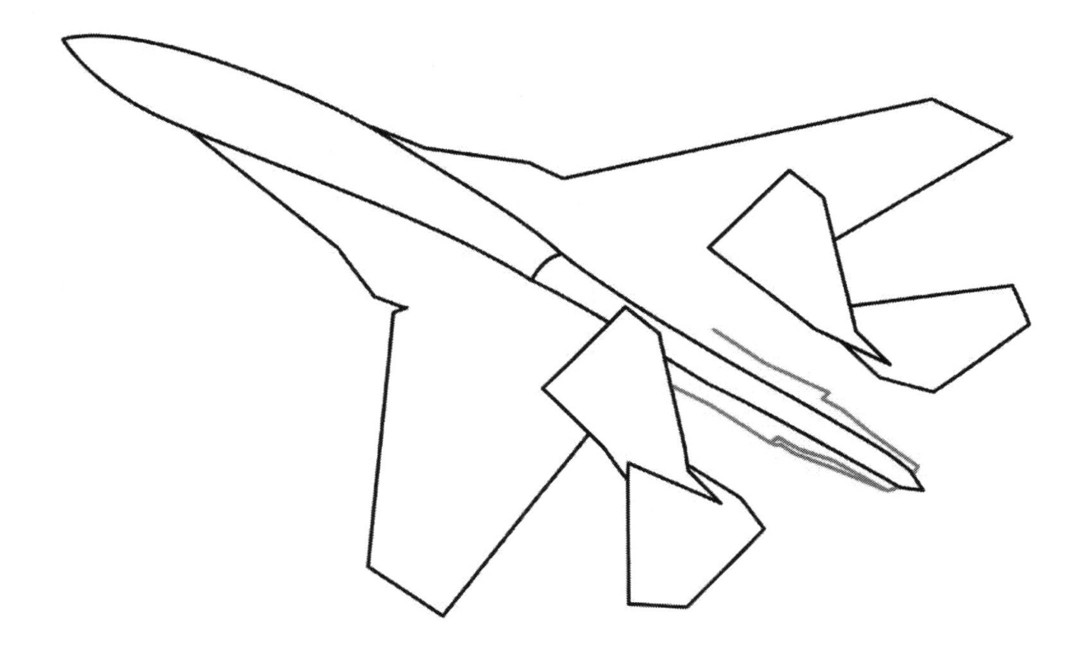

Add lines as shown in the example.

Step 8.

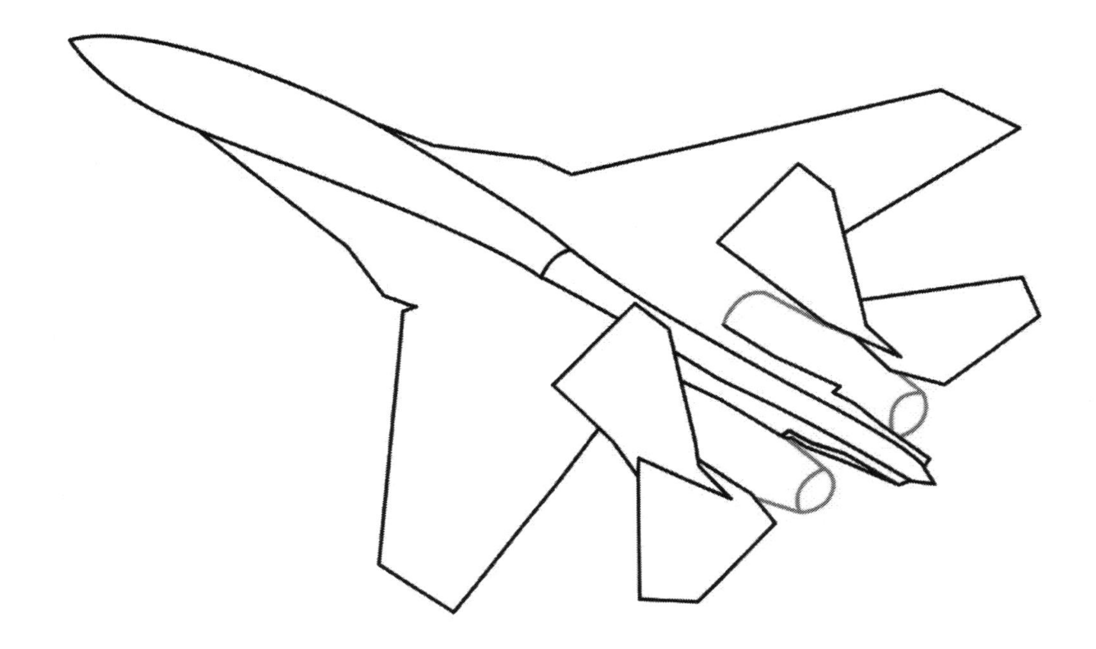

Draw large elongated turbines.

Step 9.

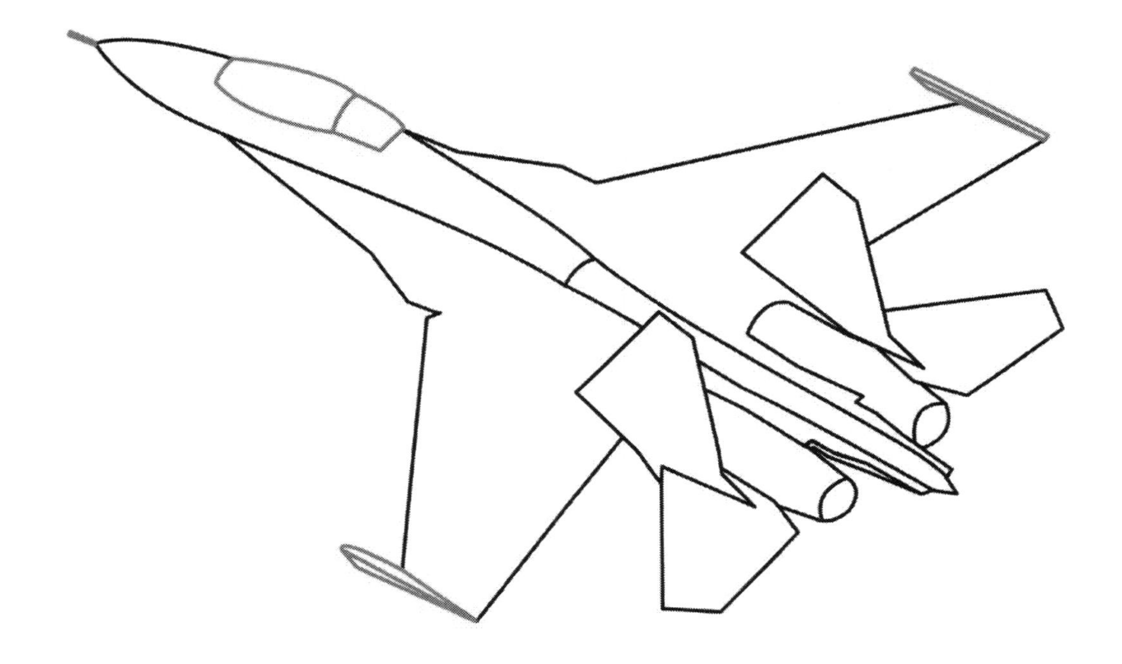

Draw the cockpit in the front upper part of the airplane, add sharp elongated parts on the nose and wings.

Step 10.

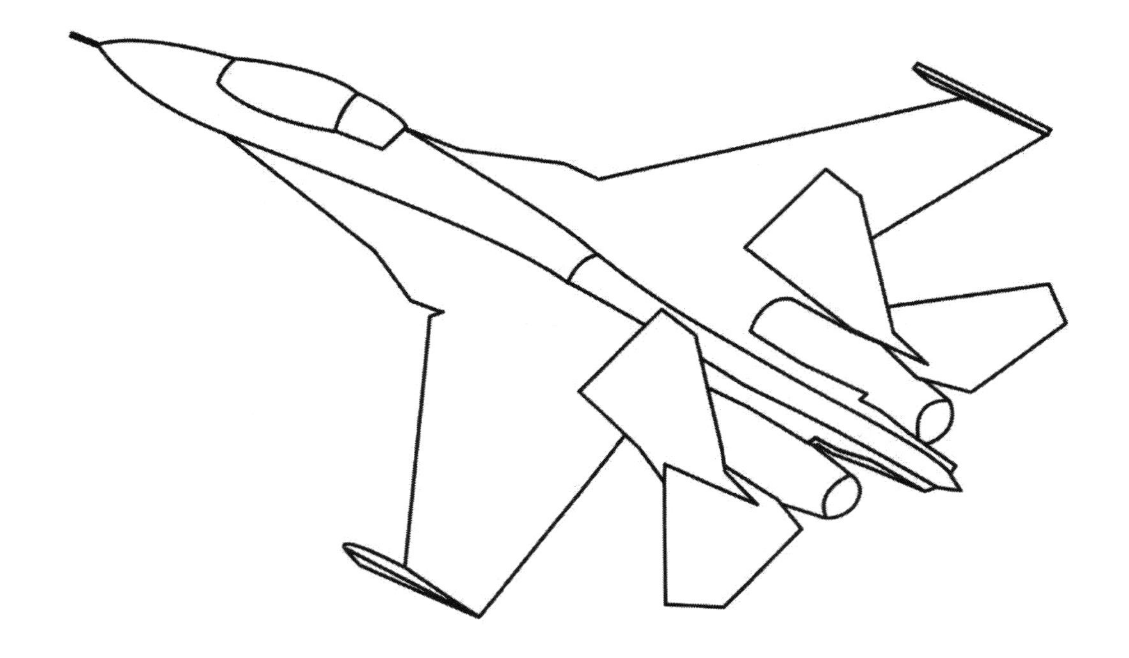

Done, let's start coloring!

Step 11.

Color picture using blue and grey for body.

Step 12.

Add some shadows and highlights to add volume.

Step 13.

Colored version.

About the Author

Andy Hopper is an American illustrator born in sunny California just a hair's breadth from the beautiful Sierra foothills. After studying Design and Media at UCLA, Andy decided to try his hand at teaching his own unique style of art to novice artists just starting out with their craft.

He has won numerous art awards and has several publications in print and e-book to his credit. His e-books teach the beginner artist how to draw using simple techniques suitable for all ages. While Andy prefers using chalk, pencil and pastels for his own artwork, but has been known to dabble in the world of watercolour from time to time and teach this skill to his students.

Andy Hopper lives just outside of Los Angeles in Santa Monica, California with his wife of 15 years and their three children. His art studio is a welcome respite to the area and he has been known to start impromptu outdoor art sessions with the people in his neighborhood for no charge.

Made in the USA
Las Vegas, NV
24 February 2021

18519685R00059